ANOREXIA NERVOSA

Learning about Anorexia

by

John Range

Table of Contents

Chapter One - Introduction 4

Chapter Two – About Anorexia 9

Chapter Three - Literature review 22

A historical frame 27

A medical/psychiatric frame 43

A sociocultural frame 49

A psychological frame 72

A philosophical frame, including religious, spiritual and
cultural factors 99

Religious, spiritual and cultural factors 112

An anthropological frame 117

Conclusion 124

Chapter One - Introduction

Self-harming behavior in youth has long been the focus of speculation and investigation. A range of activities may be attributed to the impulsivity and adventure-seeking behavior of youth, such as substance use and driving under the influence of alcohol. The daily newspapers provide numerous examples. What is harder to fathom is a young person's dangerous risk-taking where it can obviously lead to serious injury or death and why many young people deliberately cause injury to themselves.

The Youth Risk Behaviour Survey conducted in the United Kingdom by the Centre for Disease Control and Prevention in 2000 further indicates that 19.3 percent of high school students had "seriously considered attempting suicide" while nearly 15 percent had made a plan to attempt suicide.

Self-injurious behaviors, such as anorexia nervosa, cutting, and substance use have also increased significantly. With self-harming behaviors costing millions of dollars of the health budget (exact costs have not been quantified yet, according to the National Collaborating Centre for Mental Health, NCCMH) and causing immeasurable pain and grief to those affected, it has become increasingly important to understand their etiology and the context in which they are reinforced. Psychologists regard self-harm and eating disorders as separate diagnoses.

The International Classification of Diseases (ICD-10) defines anorexia nervosa as a disorder "characterized by deliberate weight loss, induced and sustained by the patient" (ICD-10).

The term "anorexia nervosa" was first used by William Gull in 1874 to mean a nervous loss of appetite. The mortality rate of anorexia nervosa is five times higher than the same aged population, thereby highlighting the urgency of tackling this problem. Indeed, anorexia nervosa has the highest mortality rate of any disorder with estimates ranging from 10 percent to 20 percent. This mortality rate is compounded by the strong link between anorexia nervosa and suicide. Current estimates indicate that 2 percent of women and 1 percent of males in Australia are afflicted by anorexia nervosa, suggesting that it is a significant problem in our society.

For this book, I use the abridged term "anorexia". Furthermore, I use the terms "disorder", "illness" and "syndrome" interchangeably, as anorexic behavior leads to a cluster of symptoms which, in their extreme form, cause "secondary endocrine and metabolic changes and disturbances of bodily function". I also use the terms "anorexic" and "anorectic" both as adjectives and nouns in the manner employed by Garrett and refer primarily to restrictive anorexia, as opposed to the purgative form. Finally, while acknowledging that anorexia afflicts both males and females, I generally use the female pronoun "she": this is for convenience primarily but also because anorexia predominantly occurs among females.

To do justice to the complexity of anorexia, I had to look beyond psychological and familial factors to the wider landscape of Western civilization and its values. The preoccupation with "body image" reflects a much deeper fixation on "image" itself.

Western societies value appearances and we might ask whether and to what extent appearances can deceive us.

While my review of the research literature demonstrates that there is no specific set of circumstances that leads to anorexia, it identifies many salient factors that appear to trigger the disorder. Although family interactions are represented as one of these salient factors, I do not consider the family primarily responsible; nor am I attributing blame. The research literature, together with my field research, continually impacted the play's development, influencing changes and additions to the first draft.

Why focus on one disorder? There are many good reasons. For instance, few plays depict this complex disorder. A play can enact a set of complicated social and familial factors that may affect the development of mental illness. It can demonstrate the types of interactions that may provide a buffer and those that may cause harm. On a broader level, I found that anorexia encapsulates many of the sociocultural forces that negatively impact upon young people, especially young women, and a play, by presenting and exploring these forces, can expose and critique potentially debilitating aspects of Western society, and especially its emphasis on body image and appearance.

Chapter Two – About Anorexia

All the researchers describe anorexia as multifactorial, with genetic, environmental, psychological, temperamental, and sociological components. Some referred to it as biopsychosocial in nature.

All professionals interviewed indicated the importance of genetic factors that appear to predispose some individuals to mental illness and make them vulnerable due to inherited temperamental and personality characteristics. Research demonstrates links between anorexia and other mental illnesses, such as anxiety and obsessive-compulsive disorder.

However, a person is more likely to develop anorexia if she or he also has the temperament or personality factors associated with this illness, such as perfectionism, rigidity, conflict avoidance, and compliant nature. It appears that while one may be born with a diathesis towards mental illness, it is one's temperament that determines the type of mental illness developed.

According to interviewees, anorexics tend to be "driven" in nature and are high achievers who strive towards perfectionism in everything they do and are disappointed in themselves if they do not live up to their expectations. One clinical psychologist also observed that anorexics often lack an "inner" life and have limited self-knowledge, describing them as "strangers" to themselves.

A health professional with a nursing background gave examples of the drive towards perfectionism that manifested in some clients. One client, for example, was unable to express herself artistically in case she did it "wrong". She was asked to dip her hand in paint and then onto a blank canvas but declined, explaining that she was afraid of making a mistake, despite being told that there were no right or wrong methods.

Not all individuals with predisposing factors develop anorexia. Health professionals emphasize the importance of environmental and situational factors. While there were some differences in opinion about factors that trigger the illness, such as the significance of familial connectedness, all agreed that environments that promote healthy self-esteem act as a buffer against developing anorexia. The corollary is that low self-esteem increases vulnerability to the illness. They described how low self-esteem affects an individual in two ways, firstly by making one more vulnerable to media depictions of body image and secondly by increasing the impact of peer influence. There is considerable documentation to support the view that individuals who lack confidence in themselves are more easily influenced by media messages and peer group pressures.

Depictions that emphasize the value of thinness result in comparisons with "ideal" images and many will find their own body wanting. Young people are typically influenced by peers who may have negative body images themselves and may emulate diet fads adopted by their friends. This combination of low self-esteem and negative body image was described by one therapist as instrumental in setting up a chain reaction that can lead to disordered eating patterns.

Another impact of low self-esteem is that individuals feel unworthy of having their basic needs met, therefore not deserving to eat. Once this belief system becomes entrenched, it is extremely hard to alter. One therapist indicated that anorexics often define their identity by their illness, making it difficult to separate themselves from the disorder. This has significant implications for recovery, as it suggests that the anorexic will cling to her illness to reinforce her sense of identity and will resist interventions that must inevitably threaten her perception of herself.

Healthy self-esteem appears to be a crucial protective shield against anorexia. However, many young people reach maturity without this buffer, thereby making them vulnerable to outside stresses. Self-esteem is cultivated through positive experiences in the home and broader social environment. Unconditional love and acceptance will strengthen a child's self-esteem while negative and critical parenting styles undermine this process. Home environments that stifle the child's voice are also detrimental to healthy self-esteem. Children whose choices or decisions are frequently belittled or countered will find more difficulty in individuating and making positive decisions in later life. They may feel that whatever they do will never be "good enough" to meet family expectations and that they must comply with certain rules or manifest certain behaviors to be loved. Unconditional love, in psychological terms, refers to love that is not determined by behavior. In this positioning, parents may disapprove of behavior without this affecting their love for the child.

One psychologist referred to the level of expressed emotion in families as another important factor in the home environment. Some parents may use highly charged language such as "this is awful", to describe an event of only moderate significance. When this type of language is directed at the child, it may be interpreted as severe criticism. On the other hand, some families may avoid expressing any emotions at all to avert potential conflicts. However, these emotions will often surface later with greater force.

Some psychologists commented on the difficulty that some parents experience in achieving the "right" balance between softness and firmness in disciplinary action. This may lead to inconsistency in the one parent or between the parents, where one of the parents is perceived as soft and the other as strict. When such parenting strategies prove to be ineffective, parents often resort to expressing themselves in a louder and more forceful manner instead of adopting a different strategy. In other words, the firm parent may attempt to alter the child's behavior by shouting more loudly, rather than trying a different tactic.

Parenting styles impact on anorexia in other ways. Parents who discourage eating certain foods can influence a person's food choice in later life, as some foods become more or less desirable depending upon the labels ascribed to them. The significance of food has a cultural basis and this also needs to be taken into account when understanding anorexia. As one of the leaders of the Bridges group pointed out, the avoidance of a particular food may represent breaking away from the client's cultural background. For this reason, it is important to know the client's ethnicity and the meanings attached to food.

Communication about food and body weight between parents also influences a child's food choices in later life. If the child witnesses one parent, usually the father, attributing excessive importance to the spouse's weight or choice of food, this may trigger fixation on their own body shape or weight.

While some of the psychologists interviewed referred to the parental disharmony and open conflict evident in many of their clients' families, they also noted that statistical analysis has shown a higher incidence of intact families compared with the general population. One therapist interpreted this to mean that such families may experience higher levels of unexpressed domestic unhappiness, and indeed many such parents tended to be more self-absorbed and preoccupied with their own problems, making them less responsive to their children's needs. While it may be argued that these observations are only anecdotal in nature, they were given by staff at an eating disorders unit that has one of the largest databases in the world and by a therapist who has treated over 900 eating disordered clients to date. In some of the cases where parental disharmony was indicated, the anorexic child appeared to use her illness to keep her parents together. In these cases, they tended to stay together to help their children and were less likely to separate or divorce.

While situations of parental or family disharmony may contribute to some cases of anorexia, most therapists expressed the view that there is no typical family structure for eating disordered clients. It appears that there are just as many over-connected as under-connected or disengaged family patterns. Families that are over-connected may inadvertently discourage the child from making decisions and becoming independent, while families that were under-connected often failed to respond to the child's needs. In the latter case, the anorexic condition focused parental attention back onto the child. While there are no clear definitions of what constitutes good parenting skills, what appears more important is the fit between the child and her relatives.

Not surprisingly, most of the professionals interviewed stressed the importance of maintaining a positive connection with one's children.

Another contributing situational factor is the instability of residence. Children who frequently moved houses experience constant disruptions to bond-formation and find it more challenging to maintain a connection with their peers. Other childhood traumas, such as sexual abuse, might also trigger anorexia, especially if the child fears maturing and eliciting further unwanted sexual interest. Bullying and teasing from one's peers also have a detrimental effect on developing self-esteem and thus increases vulnerability to an eating disorder.

One social worker described in detail the development of her own eating disorder. She had been bullied in her childhood years but later found herself to be the object of much positive male attention at high school. As a result, the girls who had bullied her now sought her friendship. This reinforced her belief that looking thin and attractive was instrumental in obtaining positive peer attention. When she began to lose weight, she received many compliments from her classmates and this further encouraged her to lose more weight, establishing a vicious circle that spiraled into anorexia.

The role of the media in promoting and reinforcing positive images of thinness was acknowledged by all professionals interviewed, except for one whose opinions will be discussed later. As one nurse pointed out, fashion magazines go to great lengths to project a distorted view of the female shape, often using techniques such as photoshopping and airbrushing to present unrealistic and impossible images of female waists that are smaller in dimension than the person's head. Apparently, one such doctored image of Kate Winslet led to her threatening legal action against the magazine for making her feel that she wasn't "good enough" in her natural state. If a celebrity of Kate Winslet's stature is offended by media representations of her body frame, it is no wonder that teenagers seeking validation in the eyes of the world are vulnerable to unrealistic depictions of the female form.

One professional, whom I shall call Annie, discounted the importance of body image as a motivating factor in anorexia. Annie works as a counselor but has lived with the anguish of witnessing her daughter's anorexia. In her view, the critical factor in this eating disorder is control. She emphasized her daughter's inability to make decisions or take control of her life. When asked a simple question, such as her favorite color, her daughter was unable to answer on her own and would seek her mother's opinion.

Annie drew attention to the strong similarities between Obsessive-Compulsive Disorder (OCD) and anorexia, referring to research that indicated that both conditions demonstrate a low level of functioning in the part of the brain responsible for strategic planning, leading to difficulties in making quick decisions.

Interestingly, Annie indicated that the turning point in her daughter's illness came when she realized that she could no longer keep her daughter alive; in other words, she was forced to relinquish control of her daughter's life. Henceforth, it became imperative for her daughter to take responsibility for herself and her recovery ensued as a result.

Given the emphasis on "thinness" in the media, it is interesting to observe the increasing incidence of obesity in Western society. One clinical psychologist referred to the "all or nothing" extremes that prevail. In other words, the culture has become excessive.

This interviewee considered it no coincidence that anorexia and obesity had both become more prevalent in image-driven, consumerist societies.

Like Annie, she pinpointed control as a central

factor in anorexia and described scenarios in which parents had wielded too much control over a child's life. Reluctant to comment on etiology, she preferred to list preventative factors, such as high self-esteem, an absence of weight issues in the family, unconditional love, connectedness and eating together as a family.

Some interviewees alluded to the self-harming nature of anorexia. One social worker stressed the self-harming nature of anorexia, stipulating that while it might not present in this manner initially, it quickly develops into a form of self-harm when the anorexic individual moves into the denial stage of the illness and subsequently manifests behavior that parallels a slow form of suicide.

Field research sometimes provided content for the play, such as the hand painting example mentioned above; at other times, my research validated an idea that I had already developed. To clarify, many interviewees mentioned the prevalence of name changing among anorexics, for example, Annie described how important it was for her daughter to change her name when she began the recovery process, as she needed to break away from her old identity.

I discovered that one of the fundamental features of anorexia is the strong link between body image and self-esteem, which is concisely expressed in a joke I heard at the Bridges' group one evening: Knock, knock. Who's there? Nobody.

Chapter Three - Literature review

Our world view is shaped by the mental structures that govern our thought processes. These mental structures or frames are formed by our language, values, and beliefs and are significantly influenced by sociocultural and psychological factors.

To reshape or change our lives, we must first be aware of the frames that influence our thinking processes. Before examining the implications of different theories used to explain anorexia, it is important to understand the significance of the frames that we take for granted and internalize when processing information from the external world. By becoming aware of a framing process that is usually unconscious, we are better able to make changes and choose alternative frames.

Language is one of the central ways we frame our world. Many words evoke conceptual frames. These may be unconscious but even when we are aware of them and attempt to block this process, we still retain the images that the words suggest.

Even when no verbal messages are conveyed, ideas are still circulated in the form of embodied images that the child draws upon in determining his or her frame of belief. One commonly held notion projected by celebrities and others is that if we strive to achieve the perfect body, through weight reduction and other forms of beautifying ourselves, then our popularity and success will increase. In fact, we are surrounded by media messages that inform us that our ideal weight is considerably less than our current size. These messages are transmitted through various frames, such as medical, socio-cultural and philosophical.

While these frames are usually referred to as discourses, I am using the terms interchangeably, as I believe that adopting a discourse to study anorexia usually leads to a cognitive set or framing of this disorder. In other words, a doctor will adopt a medical frame to conceptualize and treat the disorder, while a psychologist will choose from a range of different psychological approaches. Media advertisements using a medical frame bombard us with messages that we should reduce the amount of fat in our diet while philosophically framed promotions inform us that we will be better people and have more fulfilling lives if we follow a recommended diet.

Interestingly, even when the frame fails to fit the facts, we might discard the facts to retain the frame.

Consequently, if we encounter successful role models who do not conform to the slender ideal, we might dismiss their significance, rather than question our beliefs. Lakoff observes that all knowledge is neurologically encoded. He reasons, therefore, that these frames are also "in the synapses of our brains, physically present in the form of neural circuitry". Despite the widely held view that the "truth will set you free", it is very difficult to dispel underlying beliefs since most of our conceptual framing is performed unconsciously. Conceptual links can also become so strongly reinforced that they persist even though often they work against our self- interest.

Frames can be manipulated by attaching an innocuous interpretation to them, so that, for example, losing extra weight cannot hurt. Sometimes, these beliefs are passed down from previous generations and have become "archetypal" values that we accept without awareness. An entrenched idea might be that losing weight is always a good outcome. As noted, attempts to expose and negate the frame are ineffectual as they only serve to evoke and reinforce its significance.

This chapter explores the many different theoretical frames used to explain and conceptualize this disorder. Theories that have gained the most prominence are psychiatric (medically-based), psychological, sociological (including feminist), philosophical and historical. However, the main causative factors of anorexia may be summarised as genetic (including biological and personality traits), familial and sociocultural. It is necessary to differentiate among factors that predispose, precipitate or perpetuate the disorder. Predisposing conditions refer to genetic factors, including personality traits such as perfectionism and obsessiveness.

Precipitant factors include environmental stresses, such as frequently shifting residence, and family issues that may include a negative view of body fat. Factors that maintain the disorder may be generated from many sources, such as sociocultural attitudes that emphasize body image and reinforce psychological insecurities. Many of these factors overlap and it is difficult to separate them in certain circumstances. For instance, a person may be born with a high sensitivity or vulnerability to some environmental stresses, but parenting styles may increase this vulnerability and therefore help perpetuate the problem.

To understand the increasing incidence of

anorexia in contemporary society, it is necessary, to begin with, a historical overview.

A historical frame

Fasting has been employed throughout the ages as a means of "subduing" the flesh to enhance spiritual development. Historical accounts show that there were many young women in Europe, during medieval times and the Renaissance (1200 to 1600 approximately), who fasted for extended periods for religious or ascetic reasons. Some of these women were later beatified as saints, such as Catherine of Siena (1347–1380) and Margaret of Cortona (1219–1246).

Fasting served the dual purpose of purifying the body and gaining control over bodily desires and needs, in effect promoting an elevated spiritual state that transcends the needs of the flesh. Self-deprivation allowed Christian women to demonstrate their piety and seek penance for their sins and was used as a strategy to become closer to God. In some cases, the only sustenance ingested by these women for extended periods was the Eucharist wafer and wine representing Christ's body and blood. Many also practiced self-flagellation and sleep deprivation, forcing themselves to lie on the hard ground with rocks as pillows. Such austerities represented sacrifices to God and it was believed that, if sustenance was not obtained on a physical level, then God must be responsible for their continued survival. Physicians in the seventeenth and eighteenth centuries wrote about these practices, which they had witnessed, as well as those from earlier times, referring to such abstinence as inedia prodigiosa (great starvation) and anorexia mirabilis, or miraculously inspired loss of appetite.

While the women believed that their sacrifices were following God's wishes, much debate ensued among clerics regarding the meaning of this behavior, that is, whether their actions were the work of God or the devil, something that many parents of modern anorexics may wonder as well.

While it would appear that anorexia mirabilis and anorexia nervosa are driven by differing motivations, some theorists, including Bell, have argued for their similarity.

Both anorexia mirabilis and anorexia nervosa result from an underlying need to establish a sense of self and represent, furthermore, the quest for female liberation from a patriarchal society. Bell argues that by conquering the needs of their bodies, these women were able to exert control over their lives, achieving autonomy as well as spiritual enlightenment. He refers to this phenomenon as holy anorexia, thereby drawing a parallel between this early religious behavior and contemporary anorexia. Like its modern-day counterpart, anorexia mirabilis was primarily a female behavior.

Both forms of fasting are influenced by the social milieu of their time, include ritualistic behaviors and the use of food as a symbolic language. Fasting may also be regarded as a ritual that creates boundaries between the pure and the impure; in whatever way these concepts are defined by society. By fasting, women react to social pressures to conform and attempt to imbue their lives with meaning, thus fulfilling an underlying spiritual need. The need for spiritual fulfillment is as strong today as it was in medieval times and continues to motivate many human endeavors as.

Bell's argument does not take into account the different ages of medieval (and later) fasting women compared to contemporary fasters, mostly described as anorexic, who are primarily adolescents. It also obscures the fact that medieval fasting was only one aspect of a wide range of austerities that included self-flagellation, scalding, and sleeping in severe conditions. Another point of difference is the underlying value system driving fasting behavior. While earlier fasting appears to be driven more by collective values that include a religious or spiritual hunger, in other words, a hunger for God, contemporary abstinence is propelled primarily by an individualistic belief system.

The first description of anorexia nervosa, although it was not called by this name, has been attributed to Simone Porta (1496–1554) who described a ten-year-old girl who had stopped eating altogether. Richard Morton, in 1694, is credited with giving the first detailed description of the symptoms of anorexia nervosa, which he called phthisis Nervosa, meaning nervous atrophy or nervous consumption. However, Morton described only some of the symptoms of anorexia nervosa and was unaware that the illness was predominantly an adolescent female condition. Many other symptoms given in his account do not fit the current definition of anorexia nervosa. Morton, however, was describing a very small sample size whose fasting may have been compounded by other factors.

By the seventeenth and eighteenth centuries, and corresponding with the rise of the Protestant Reformation, fasting was actively discouraged as it was regarded as the work of Satan and not of God. Where once it had been viewed as a form of female holiness, it was now seen as heretical and even bordering on insanity. Despite this widely held view, fasting behavior lingered on, coexisting with Protestant iconoclasm through the sixteenth to nineteenth centuries. Many of these women came under the scrutiny of clerics and medical practitioners who found that several of them were fraudulent, as they were secretly ingesting nourishment.

In 1859, William Chipley published the first American description of sitomania which was characterized by an "intense dread of food". However, this condition was classified as a subcategory of insanity and does not meet our current understanding of the disorder. Anorexia nervosa was first medically named and described in the 1870s by professionals in England, France, and America. The principal doctors credited with defining anorexia nervosa were William Gull, a physician from England, and French neurologist Charles Lasegue, who independently gave detailed accounts of the illness, although the latter considered it to be a variant of hysteria. Gull's definition of anorexia nervosa, implicated a "moral or mental aberration rooted in the nervous system but exacerbated by the patient's age, her mode of life or both". He initially referred to the disorder as "apepsia hysterica" but later adopted the title anorexia nervosa.

The first cases of anorexia nervosa were observed in middle class, respectable and upwardly mobile families, leading many medical practitioners and theorists of the 1870s to conclude that anorexia was a by-product of particular social conditions. Characterized by material comfort, the sexual division of labor and stratified divisions of gender and class, the bourgeois lifestyle of the nineteenth century marked the birth of contemporary eating disorders, in particular anorexia, further indicating that this disorder is primarily associated with the way women have been conceptualized in Western culture. Secularisation is the movement of a society from a religious to a non-religious world view, while medicalization refers to the process by which scientific medicine becomes the basis of understanding human behavior.

During the transitional stage of the nineteenth century, food refusal led to priests and physicians arguing about who had the correct interpretation of this behavior. As the medical viewpoint gained prominence, the interpretation of food refusal changed from its being considered a religious act to a pathological state. As most of the known cases of food refusal came from the upper echelons of society, medical practitioners regarded anorexia as another type of nervous disorder which prevailed in the middle to higher classes of social strata.

As the majority of middle-class children lived at home until they married, dependency on their families was sometimes prolonged and intensified relationships between parents and children. This contrasted with working-class families, whose children were sometimes forced, for financial reasons, to live and work away from the family home. Lasegue presented the first detailed insight into this type of pressurized family environment, where food refusal had great power to disrupt family life and contribute to intrafamilial conflict. Middle-class girls were expected to make appropriate and, if possible, advantageous marriages, and were under constant pressure to conform and behave respectably.

Given the emotional constraints of her upbringing, the Victorian girl had few choices if she wanted to rebel against family pressures and expectations. Food refusal and ultimately anorexia became a means to express some autonomy.

Another factor in the emergence of anorexia in Victorian society was that women who were unable to express their unhappiness in any other manner used physical complaints as a form of self-expression. They would adopt the so-called privileged "sick" role, allowing them to retreat from unwanted social duties. This also became the basis of "hysteria", a condition that led to the development of Freudian psychoanalysis. As the prevalent diseases of the era involved some form of "wasting", anorexia fitted the medical stereotype perfectly. Furthermore, social etiquette demanded frugality in eating as it was considered vulgar to overload one's dinner plate. Women were required to demonstrate delicacy in their manners at all times and would eat sparingly in social situations. Overeating was not only the pathway to physical ugliness but had moral overtones as well.

Appetite became the "barometer of a woman's moral state" and restricted eating implied a higher spiritual focus.

In this regard, medieval ascetic behavior and Victorian social etiquette both positioned indulgence on a physical level as a contraindication of spiritual and sexual purity. Comparable to medieval asceticism, restraint suggested a conquering of bodily desires, indicating purity and the capacity to make sacrifices. From this point, it was only a short step to equating beauty with saintliness. A beautiful woman was saint-like and, inversely, the saintly were considered beautiful.

A thin, delicate frame was not only an object of beauty but also indicated social status because of its unsuitability for productive or even reproductive work. Manual laboring requires a more robust constitution than that which typified the upper-middle classes and, in this way, body size became an indicator of social status. Women from elite society demonstrated their distance from the working classes by their slenderness. By controlling their appetites, Victorian women were able to express "emotional, aesthetic and class sensibilities" and women of means from this era were the first to diet, long before the fashion trends of the 1920s and 1960s. Thus, it appears that the seeds of the twentieth century's obsession with body image, as opposed to body function, which continues into the twenty-first century, were sown in the Victorian climate of respectability.

An association between the rising incidence of anorexia and the rise of capitalism and affluence in many post-industrial societies has been widely documented. Some have even called the difficulties generated by the capitalist system consumption disorders, arguing that in a society in which one's identity is to some extent defined by what one consumes, non-consumption is also a signifier of identity. Indeed it can be argued that, in a consumerist society, the non-consumer can make a very powerful statement.

If anorexia only develops under conditions of emotional and material privilege, then the increasing affluence of the Western world in the 1900s would appear to guarantee a surge in the incidence of eating disorders. According to research, 90 to 95 percent of anorectics are young, female, white and from middle and upper-class families. Anorexia occurs in a context of plenty and is not observed in periods of food restriction and famine.

Food refusal would be an ineffectual tool in a setting of poverty and food scarcity, especially if food refusal is viewed as the adolescent's struggle with autonomy, individuation and sexual development. On a more general level, it has been suggested that corpulence is valued when times are lean and women are needed to procure food, while thinness is valued more when biological survival is not threatened and women are expected to pursue more intellectual, aesthetic and spiritual goals. It has been argued that by the twentieth-century obesity was no longer just a physical liability but had become a social impediment and character flaw. However, this applies to affluent Western society only, as in many other cultures obesity represents wealth and power.

Victorian medical practitioners never presented explanations for food refusal, for most of them failed to interview their patients about this behavior. They also failed to understand the connection between anorexia and the cultural milieu of the time, regarding it more as a perversion of will or a form of attention-seeking behavior. It was not until the turn of the twentieth century that Janet, a key figure in hysteria studies, first differentiated between two types of anorexia: obsessional and hysterical. Patients with obsessional anorexia, while still retaining their hunger, presented with a horror of eating, gaining weight and developing a woman's body. In contrast, patients with hysterical anorexia found it impossible to eat, regurgitated any food ingested and were hyperactive.

In the first couple of decades of the twentieth century, anorexia was often confused with other forms of mental illness, such as depression and psychosis. From the 1920s through to the 1930s, and endocrinologic approach was primarily adopted in the treatment of anorexia. Despite a lack of evidence, this approach targeted the thyroid, ovaries, pituitary or pancreatic regions. Simultaneously, psychogenic factors were explored by practitioners, such as Freud (1856–1939) and Janet (1859–1947), who were the first theorists to link appetite loss to sexuality. While Freud's treatment of anorexia was sparse and he made only passing observations that anorexia was a form of melancholia linked to undeveloped sexuality, his greatest contribution lay in asking about the underlying meaning of anorexia. He saw the anorectic's rejection of food as intrinsically associated with sexuality and a rejection of it. Similarly, Janet linked anorexia to the anorectic's unconscious desire to remain a young girl by blocking the development of womanly features, thereby suggesting a psychosexual etiology.

In the 1930s, anorexia was widely considered a neurotic or psychological disorder predominantly associated with females. While biomedical approaches were still employed, psychotherapy became the preferred form of treatment. This approach resulted in the observation of commonalities among anorectics, such as superior intelligence and drivenness. Once again, the link between anorexia and sexuality was indicated with some anorexic patients expressing a fear that eating would lead to pregnancy.

Psychoanalytic interpretations of anorexia in the 1930s revolved around the assumption that oral disturbances, related to breast-feeding, characterized the disorder. This further implicated the mother-child relationship and raised the idea that the child develops resentment against the mother if her needs for nurturance are not adequately fulfilled. Anorexia provides the child with a state of independence that does not require anyone else to fulfill their needs. Mother-child relationships were later explored by Palazzoli who argued that overprotective mothering increased the risk factor of developing anorexia.

Psychosomatic medicine in the 1930s and 1940s, with its emphasis on the relationship between mind and body, posited anorexia as an illness that linked personality disorders with somatic functions. In the context of mind/body dualism, anorexia can be regarded as a triumph of the mind over the body. It was not until Bruch's work, post World War 2, that the full complexity of the disorder was traced back to the developmental history of the individual. Rather than a loss of appetite, anorexia came to be understood as suppression of appetite, resulting from a complicated set of psychological and cultural factors. Further analysis of these factors will be presented later in this chapter.

Ironically, an increasing incidence of anorexia since the beginning of the twentieth century coincides with the feminist movement. Beginning with the suffragette movement in the UK in 1872, women used hunger strikes to rally for equality of rights and opportunities. While this form of food refusal was never considered anorexic, it arguably created a context for women to use food to express their autonomy. With the first wave of feminism in the 1920s, the slim, straight, almost boyish look of the flapper became synonymous with beauty and again, in the 1960s, the stick-thin image of Twiggy was promoted as ideal. Interestingly, in Australia, most of the women's magazines that glorified this ideal body image had female editors, although they often worked for male bosses.

The shift in cultural ideology from the twelfth to the twentieth century can be understood in the context of a movement from spiritual aspirations to physical ideals. Rather than striving for spiritual holiness, women's focus was directed to the attainment of a physical image that was promoted by the emergence of capitalism through the fashion and cosmetics industries, beauty pageants, the modeling profession and the rise of cinema.

As a result, the distinction between the sacred and secular has blurred and a decrease in conventional religious practices has led to women seeking solutions to life's problems in popular culture.

A medical/psychiatric frame

The medical theory of anorexia dates back to 1873 when both William Gull and Charles Lasegue gave accounts of the illness. Contemporary medical theory positions anorexia as a serious biologically-based mental illness (BBMI) that is "significantly heritable" and influenced by changes in brain functioning. A BBMI is defined as a condition caused by a "neurobiological disorder of the brain" who cite twin studies, indicating that 50 to 83 percent of variance in anorexia and other eating disorders can be explained by genetic factors, meaning that these disorders contain a significant genetic predisposition.

Genetic loadings predispose the individual to develop anorexia through biological abnormalities and personality traits. They further indicate that chromosomal regions and genes have been identified as risk factors in the development of anorexia. Specifically, the genes responsible for the creation of serotonin, brain-derived neurotrophic factor (BDNF) and opioid systems appear to be associated with anorexia.

Furthermore, there is an endocrine disorder "affecting the hypothalamic-pituitary-gonadal axis" that impacts appetite regulation, satiety, and eating. While the nature of this disorder remains unclear, it may lead to abnormal sensitivities in some individuals. However, it is difficult to disentangle the relationship between the endocrine system and anorexia, as symptoms of anorexia, such as weight loss and increased exercise, may cause changes in the endocrine system.

As eating is controlled both peripherally, in the stomach, and centrally, by the hypothalamus, there appears to be a complex interaction between the two control centers, complicated further by changes that are due to the starvation process itself. This relationship was explored in an experiment on the effects of semi-starvation conducted in Minnesota during World War 2. War conditions were simulated by giving a group of young men a severely restricted diet. As cited by Bruch, this led to the men demonstrating behaviors similar to anorexics, such as obsessive preoccupation with food, self-absorption and child-like regression. As a result, it is difficult to establish whether such factors predispose an individual to anorexia or whether they are a result of the condition developing. The widely accepted view is that endocrine changes are a result of anorexia behaviors and not the cause of them.

Serotonin activity, however, appears to predate

the onset of the disorder and may predispose the individual to anorexia and other eating disorders. Serotonin is a neurotransmitter that enables an organism to tolerate delay. While low levels of serotonin activity are linked to impulsivity, which has also been linked to bulimia, high levels of serotonin are associated with rigidity and constraint that have in turn been linked with anorexia. This has been further indicated by Klump, et al. who have observed profound disturbances of brain serotonin, neuropeptide systems, and brain neurocircuitry which are still present following recovery from anorexia. Brain circuits that control appetite, mood, cognitive function, and impulse control are all implicated.

The biological basis of eating disorders is supported to some extent by animal research. Anorexic phenotypes, such as decreased food intake and high activity levels, have been observed in rodents that have autosomal recessive mutations or gene alterations, suggesting that anorexia also has a biological profile. Klump concludes that neurobiological abnormalities are evident in both the illness phase and post-recovery from the disorder. While many of the abnormalities found in brain structure and function are secondary to weight loss and reverse with weight restoration, the unilateral reduction of blood flow in the anterior position of the temporal lobe observed in children and adolescents with anorexia suggests a primary abnormality in the limbic system.

The strong links between belief systems and relevant neurological pathways have been explored in recent research that indicates that our perceptions leave a physiological map in our brain structure and that this process further reinforces our belief. What we believe shapes the neuronal structure of our brain which, in turn, shapes our experiences of the world. The anorexic perceives her body to be fat because that is the image that has been processed on her brain map and according to Bach-y-Rita, "We see with our brains, not with our eyes."

Previous thinking, dating back to Descartes, conceptualized mind and body as a duality, which led to confusion about how our minds could influence our bodies when they were composed of completely different substances. Research into neuroplasticity explains this phenomenon by suggesting that our thoughts and our imaginings alter our brain maps: "Everything your 'immaterial' mind imagines leaves material traces. Each thought alters the physical state of your brain synapses at a microscopic level". The longer the perceptual frame has been held, the harder it is to change the behavior as the internal map becomes embedded in brain structure. Distorted body image clearly demonstrates that there is a distinct difference between the perception of body shape and actual size. While many individuals with a distorted body image elect for plastic surgery, what they actually need is "neuroplastic surgery" to correct their body image.

Recent research indicates that people with eating disorders show functional abnormalities in brain systems that process body image. People with eating disorders exhibit relatively low levels of activity in some neural networks such as the right parietal cortex. Research examining the neural correlates associated with underlying state and trait characteristics of anorexia suggests that medial prefrontal neural activity is linked to a vulnerability trait associated with the illness. Summarising research into the molecular genetic basis of eating disorders.

Anorexia has also been linked with psychiatric conditions, such as depression, anxiety disorders, and OCD, with up to 80 percent of anorexics diagnosed with additional disorders. As these illnesses carry significant genetic and biological risk factors, this finding further supports the theory of a genetic and biological basis for anorexia.

After examining all the medical research, many theorists have concluded that anorexia, like other BBMI conditions, has multifactorial causes, indicating that environmental circumstances interact with genetic, biological and temperamental factors that predispose the individual to develop this condition. This further supports the view that the medical and psychiatric approaches alone cannot fully explain the complexities of anorexia.

A sociocultural frame

"A woman can never be too rich or too thin".

The above aphorism, attributed to the Duchess of Windsor, encapsulates the social view of women from the turn of the twentieth century until the present. It suggests, in a humorous manner, the importance of body size and wealth in determining women's destinies. Sociological theory positions anorexia in a cultural context in three different ways: the importance of a thin body in itself; the significance of appearance in the female role and; the central importance of appearance for societal success.

As discussed, sociocultural frames are extremely powerful in shaping our world view because they act on an unconscious level. As some theorists have pointed to a link between the rise of feminism and an increase in eating disorders, I also consider the possible implications of feminist movements for anorexia. It should be noted that there is a distinct difference between healthy slimness and the extreme thinness that anorexics strive towards. In this section, it is the latter form of thinness that is concerning.

Children learn from a very young age that body

size is important and that thinness is a highly valued attribute in contemporary Western societies. From receiving their first gift of a Barbie doll, with its physically impossible body dimensions, to watching fashion pageants and reading magazines, such as *Girlfriend*, that specifically target pre-teens, or tweens as they are now called, the developing child is bombarded with images of a thin- ideal that is unattainable for most women.

The advertising industry and the media depict images of the ideal body, upholding celebrity role models, many of whom, extol the virtues of dieting. Children as young as five have competed in beauty pageants in America for some time, but recently a pageant known as *Toddlers in Tiaras* was staged in Australia. Mass protests outside venues in Australia indicate that people are becoming more aware of the inherent dangers of these events. Pageants such as these, while not necessarily emphasizing thinness per se, introduce children to the importance of appearance, even before they have learned the value of education.

Body image has become laden with moral overtones so that slimness is equated with "restraint, moderation and self-control" and obesity with self-indulgence and greed. As a consequence, many women have come to equate self-worth with their weight and consider that "a thin woman is a 'valued' woman". This has had a profound influence on children, with 70 percent of nine-year-old San Franciscans dieting because they perceive themselves as too fat and 50 percent of six-year-old Canadian girls not wanting to wear bathing suits or visit the beach as they feel too self-conscious about their bodies.

Many teens and tweens read magazines and peruse the internet to keep up with the latest fashions, ensuring that they don't inadvertently make a fashion blunder when catching up with their friends. A mistake in presentation could result in a lowering of their social status from "cool" to "uncool" and shift them from the "in-crowd" to a less popular group. Some tweens choose friends based on what they wear. For those with unrestricted access to digital technologies that allow social contact twenty-four hours per day, peer influence has never been greater.

This new generation has been described as tribal, and some theorists have postulated that peers have become a second family to many young people. The need to conform to the right image exerts pressure on parents to purchase expensive brand products, thereby creating a lucrative market for many manufacturers, who, in turn, target the tween population in their advertising. With such an emphasis on brand products, some tweens base their identity on what they buy and how they look. This fosters a "pack mentality" where social acceptance and belonging becomes much more important than individual expression.

Ironically, these same young people believe that they are different from their peers and make their own choices, indicating that they value uniqueness. Furthermore, while most children experience similar pressures to conform, many can negotiate these stresses and avoid severe disorders.

Young children are currently exposed to the media on an unprecedented level, leading some theorists to observe that children spend less time with their parents than watching advertisements. Media influences now supplant the role of parents in shaping the next generation.

One effect of early exposure to the media and social networking sites, such as Facebook, is that some girls are growing up too quickly and becoming sexualized too young. Before they have a chance to discover who they are and what they want to achieve in life, they are identifying themselves primarily with their body image and their attractiveness. According to the World Health Organisation, puberty occurs earlier now than in the past. Although it is unclear why this is happening, it appears that obesity and exposure to environmental chemicals are indicated.

With research from the UK in 2000 demonstrating that 16 percent of girls reach puberty by the age of eight, there is an increasing disparity between brain development and the physical, cognitive and emotional levels of maturity. While many girls are biologically mature at a young age, they are not psychologically or socially ready for the implications of their physical development. Recent brain research supports the notion that girls' brains are maturing faster than boys' brains, with approximately 30 percent more connections appear at the same age. However, this research also indicates that the prefrontal cortex, which is responsible for reasoning and problem solving, matures last. This means that girls may be prone to act impulsively and cannot make sound decisions.

According to some theorists, adolescence is a relatively new phenomenon deriving from changes in work patterns that resulted from the Industrial Revolution. Previously, young people moved from childhood to adulthood without having an in-between stage as they were deemed old enough to take paid work or raise a family.

Adolescence is the stage when young people adjust to physical changes in their bodies as well as learning to individuate and separate from parental control. Some theorists have noted that girls are progressing from "toys to boys" and rejecting childhood images at an early age, for instance, Pokemon characters, are replaced by adult images such as popstar posters that are characterized by their unhealthy emphasis on body image. Research in the United Kingdom shows that a significant number of seven- to eleven-year-old girls are expressing hostility to Barbie dolls that they had received in earlier childhood and are even dismembering and decapitating them in their rejection of childhood toys. Of course, it could be argued that they are also unconsciously rejecting the Barbie-doll image! More research needs to be conducted to clarify exactly what this means in terms of children's development.

Many young girls seek to emulate pop celebrities, such as Beyonce, Britney Spears or Lady Gaga, wearing provocative and revealing outfits that elicit male attention.

Hamilton suggests that, as a result, many girls enter intense sexual relationships at a very young age.

What is clearer though is that a loss of connectedness within the extended family and a breakdown in traditional social institutions that cemented the community together have resulted in social fragmentation, causing young people to bond more with peers than older people who, in the past, acted as role models. While there were also negative, socially oppressive forces in traditional society, including the belief that women did not need education as their role was to marry and raise children, I am primarily focusing on the issue of connectedness within traditional and modern societies.

This modern trend has been referred to as a "crisis in connection", with some girls believing that they have to risk personal safety by achieving extreme thinness and some engaging in sexual activity and drug-taking to be accepted by their social network. High rates of family breakdown and divorce, currently estimated at approximately 50 percent of all marriages, have contributed further to this process. While peer bonds can also be a positive factor, validating and supporting a young person's development, I am primarily referring to those which encourage unhealthy behavior.

Peer groups exert a powerful influence on all levels from a choice of make-up and clothes to values and beliefs. Carr-Gregg outlines the various hierarchical roles existing in female cliques, that is, queen bees, messengers, floaters, torn bystanders, pleasers and targets where the queen bee exerts tremendous power over other girls who feel that they must conform to her image and behavior or face ostracism from the group. Intense fear of social isolation might result in the majority of girls conforming to the values of the group, which determines whom they interact with, what subjects they choose at school, which boyfriend is suitable, and more importantly for this book, what appearance they choose. All of these factors are inter-related and often determine the girl's future pathway.

While there may be underlying resentments and antagonisms in a group, these are not openly expressed to other members of the group. Instead, they may be expressed at home, where the teenager may feel it is safe to take out her frustrations on her family. With such high pressure to conform to the values and norms of her peer group, it is no wonder that the struggle for identity may become a battlefield. Peer group dynamics exert a powerful, and sometimes, destructive influence.

Sociocultural definitions of what constitutes desirable attributes in women have changed dramatically through the ages and vary across cultures. Ancient goddess-worshipping cultures that have left behind figurines, such as the Venus of Willendorf, 25,000 BCE, depict women who were both obese and pregnant, suggesting that they may have linked obesity with sexuality and fertility.

Even in early Victorian times, plumpness was considered attractive, with artistic portrayals of women emphasizing "lush" fertility, which was described as women's silken layer. Indeed, it can be argued that until the twentieth century, only women with large breasts and broad hips, which signify their reproductive ability, were regarded as beautiful. Slimness only came into vogue on a widespread level during the period 1918 to 1925 and from the 1960s. The earlier period was associated with women being granted the vote, particularly in Australia, and entering the workforce in larger numbers.

With the advent of World War 2 and many more women needed to fill what had been traditionally male roles in the workforce, the struggle for equal rights, conditions and pay led to the proposal of an Equal Rights Amendment (ERA) in the US in the 1940s. After the war, the media, social pressure and governmental policy urged women to return to domestic duties, freeing up positions in the workforce for returning male soldiers. Although many did return to the home front, as it was known during war times, the women's movement and feminism were established as a major social force by the 1960s, encouraging women to re-enter the workforce and educational institutions in unprecedented numbers.

Many men, whose traditional power base centered on employment, felt that their positions were threatened and undermined by the increased numbers of women entering what had been traditionally male domains. With the ERA proposal protecting women's rights in the workforce, they turned the focus of their attack on the women's movement. This attack or backlash against feminism centered primarily upon women's appearance. At the same time, the market place, which had previously directed its attention to domestic women and the sale of household and fashion products, was forced to change its focus to stay in business. After World War 2, with war contracts coming to an end, a market focusing on household appliances and other "feminine mystique" products, as they came to be known, had surfaced in the 1950s. With increasing numbers of women entering the workforce, this market shifted towards the production of new and different beauty products to ensure the survival of these companies. Given that working women require professional clothing, the new market shifted its focus from fashion to the body itself, and a new industry that centered on women's beauty was born.

Magazines and other media forums that had previously focused on fashion and household products created a new market that centered primarily on re-modeling the body. This new market comprised an annual $32 billion thinness industry and $20 billion youth industry in the 1990s and was based on diet, fitness, skincare and surgery. Women who had been beginning to gain confidence in their abilities as a result of their achievements in the workforce were now undermined by this new pressure to conform to beauty standards propagated by a changing market economy.

The backlash against feminism took another more sinister turn by questioning women's femininity and beauty. Feminists were described in popular culture and the media as ugly or failed women, with some media forums suggesting that they had only become activists because they were too repulsive to find a husband.

This emphasis on women's appearance also led to the subtle but subversive implementation of criteria in job selection processes that contained references to appearance, a criterion that has been called the Professional Beauty Quotient (PBQ). PBQ has been used in the hiring and firing of women across many professions where their male counterparts are not judged by their level of attractiveness. With increasing attention on beauty, women's body shape and size came under closer scrutiny and a new phenomenon of "weightism" was born. Weightism has been described as a form of prejudice negatively affecting both thin and obese people and has the effect of sabotaging women's success and achievement. While women were striving to achieve in the workforce, the emphasis on thinness became part of the backlash directed against them.

With women becoming increasingly fixated on their appearance, a thriving industry based on beauty products dominated the market place. To ensure its economic survival, it played upon women's fears and anxieties about their body image, thereby ensuring that women continued to be the predominant consumers of their products. It was not the first time that women's beauty was used as a form of currency, with some theorists believing that beauty has come to be evaluated as wealth in our consumer economy. A popular aphorism describing women as looking like a million dollars exemplifies this association between beauty and wealth. Many industries thrive on the "beauty myth".

Cosmetics and cosmetic surgery have become huge money-spinners in the current zeitgeist with women feeling that they must reshape their faces and bodies to improve upon nature, believing that they are not good enough in their natural form.

Plastic surgery has become a thriving business in America, Australia, the United Kingdom, and many other nations but when it first proliferated in America in the 1960s, it led to an over-supply of plastic surgeons on the market. After consulting with each other, they initiated a massive advertising campaign that was pitched at women's insecurities about their physical appearance. This resulted in an escalating demand for plastic surgery and launched the highly lucrative market that it has become recently. While much of this demand is for breast augmentation and lip enlargement, the market includes facial reconstruction and the removal of fat.

Despite the relatively high risk of complications that have become evident in this field, women willingly put themselves under the knife to improve facial features and remove unwanted fat. This is not surprising when research demonstrates that 44 percent of adult women in the United States are currently dieting and 80 percent do not like the way they look. In the adolescent world, 80 percent of girls aged 13 are dieting and, with younger children, the scenario does not improve. Research shows that 81 percent of ten-year-olds feared being fat and 46 percent of girls aged 9 to 11 are dieting. With the bulk of women's magazines being driven by advertising, it is difficult for women to separate genuine pro-women content from the "beauty myth" which is primarily economic in motivation.

Recent research has investigated the link between mass media, negative body image, and disordered eating, with research finding that the mass media is saturated with unhealthy messages. Furthermore, it has been shown that there is a significant positive correlation between the level of exposure to mass media and body dissatisfaction, internalization and disordered eating. By early adolescence, the causal risk factor is not so much media exposure or internalization of the thin-ideal, but the core beliefs and assumptions held by the individual about the importance of appearance in one's life. Of course, it can also be argued that media exposure impacts upon beliefs and assumptions.

It is very concerning that these mental frames have already been established by early adolescence. Other research has examined the effects of pro-ana (pro-anorexia) websites, but as most individuals accessing these sites have a pre-existing disorder, a causal link has not been established. Based on a comprehensive overview of the research, it was concluded that the mass media is best viewed as a variable risk factor.

Employing a social psychological lens, they explore the impact and effectiveness of mass media images by examining four different social psychological theories: cultivation theory, gratification and uses theory, social comparison theory, and objectification theory. Cultivation theory examines the cumulative nature and frequency of messages depicted in the media, with the view that the more media exposure the individual has, the more mass media images are seen as realistic. In other words, the more that images of thin-ideal body shapes are linked with success and beauty, the more likelihood there is of disordered eating.

Furthermore, a barrage of these images results in women believing that by changing their behavior and dieting, they can attain these ideals, namely, success and beauty. However, this theory does not address women's resistance to these images, since only a small percentage of women exposed to them develop severe body dissatisfaction or eating disorders, although, of course, their self-esteem may still be affected.

Uses and gratification theory centers on the role of individuals in terms of how they choose to interpret and react to images. The argument here is that while the frequency and content of mass media images have an influence, it is mediated by a woman's sense of body image. It has been argued that the more dissatisfied one is with one's body before media exposure, the more dissatisfied they become after exposure. Social comparison theorists postulate that individuals strive to improve themselves, compare themselves to others and in particular compare themselves with those who are similar to them. Social comparisons regarding physical appearance are usually upward in that women will compare themselves with women they deem more attractive, which causes more negative self-perceptions of attractiveness.

However, this theory fails to consider a wider cultural umbrella and assumes that white, middle-class women are the norm. Objectification theory deals with the intrinsic nature of media images of the body, such as the many images sexually objectifying women's bodies or portraying them as thin, beautiful and fragmented body parts. Sexual objectification socializes women to see themselves as objects that are evaluated by their appearance. Girls learn from a young age that looks matter and that judgments on their appearance will affect social and economic life outcomes. As a result, girls may become preoccupied with their appearance to anticipate and control this treatment of themselves. This leads to a process of self-objectification that incurs many emotional and behavioral consequences.

Body image is the image held of the body in the individual's mind. Some theorists have used the term in a broader way to refer to the psychological domain where body, mind, and culture merge. As it is a construct of the imagination, it should not be confused with the actual physical body that an observer sees. Our relationship with our bodies is central to our relationship with ourselves and others and, when it is acutely negative, it is associated with disordered eating, low self-esteem and some forms of depression.

The link between negative body image and anorexia has long been upheld by research, with a proliferation of clinical publications in body image research increasing alongside eating disorder research. Factors that influence body image are wide-ranging, from the nature of family expressiveness to broader sociological frameworks but, significantly, body image has been linked to identity development and self-concept. Women with lower self-esteem were more likely to be concerned about and conform to societal expectations.

They were also more likely to base their sense of self-worth on their body weight. All of these factors are associated with the internalization of societal standards of attractiveness. It can be argued that individuals with a less clear sense of their own identity refer to external sources to help define themselves and, as such, become more vulnerable to the impact of media representations of thin-ideals. Not surprisingly, research has found that females are more likely than males to internalize societal standards of attractiveness when this is defined by thin-ideal images.

If sociocultural pressures to be thin are linked to anorexia, then it would appear that particular hobbies and professions, such as dancing and modeling, would show a greater representation of dieting concerns and anorexia. Research has found that there is a significantly higher representation of anorexia in dance and modeling groups and that those groups with a higher level of competitiveness showed a higher incidence of anorexia. Another cultural construct associated with anorexia is gender roles. As previously outlined, men are usually judged for their mental prowess, while women have been traditionally valued for their bodies and attractiveness to men. Research has indicated an association between feminity and eating disorders.

Characteristics deemed feminine on the Bem Sex-Role Inventory (BSRI), such as a need for approval, low self-esteem, and submissive behaviors, are significantly related to the development and severity of eating disorder symptoms. The BSRI measures psychological masculinity and femininity. Furthermore, research shows that patients with eating disorders rate much higher on feminine traits than female university students without eating problems, 42.9 percent compared with 23.8 percent in the latter group. It could be argued that the two sample groups were not comparable, as one group consisted of students and the other of patients. In research conducted in 2003, Behar found that restricting anorexics (those that limited food intake) had the highest percentage on the feminine category of the BSRI.

Femininity is the main trait of gender identity in patients suffering from restrictive anorexia; in other words, these types of anorexics conform more than other females to the feminine role. In this manner, gender traits provide a way of studying the sociocultural context of behaviors and attitudes.

Other discourses extrapolate on the role of gender by noting that the feminine role is to provide food for others while often restraining her own food intake and, on a broader level, to fulfill others' needs while denying her own. Once again, this statement generalizes and does not take into account women who do not conform to this role. In this way, the anorectic response becomes a means of conforming to the expected feminine role, while at the same time, rebelling against it to regain some control over one's body and life.

Stice's overview of the risk factors in eating disorders points to perceived pressure for thinness, thin-ideal internalization, body dissatisfaction, dietary restraint, negative affect or emotions, and substance use, with body dissatisfaction and dietary restraint being prodromal stages in the development of eating disorders. Prodromes are defined as early symptoms that indicate the onset of a psychiatric condition.

An understanding of prodromal features is critical in developing interventions and prevention programs for eating disorders. Those interventions that focus on reducing thin-ideal internalization, body dissatisfaction, and negative affect have been shown to significantly reduce eating disorder symptoms. Two social pressures put women at risk of eating disorders; the emphasis on thinness as a precondition for attractiveness and the conflict between traditional and non- traditional roles.

In contemporary society, women strive to be good wives and mothers while also striving to achieve academic and career success, with very little support offered to them while trying to balance both roles. The attempt to achieve often unobtainable goals, such as unrealistic ideals of thinness or success, impacts negatively upon women's mental health, and women who have internalized sociocultural expectations of them are more likely to develop eating disorders. These factors could, in part, explain the relationship between the rise of feminism and the proliferation of eating disorders, although there is no clear evidence for this at present.

A psychological frame

Anorexics often find themselves ensnared and controlled by forces above and beyond them, unable to take charge of their lives. Only through their disorder, do they achieve a sense of control or authority. It is as if, in hunger, they can discover their inner kingdom, and I found this a useful metaphor to understand how powerful hunger is to the anorexic.

Several different psychological approaches help to explain the development of anorexia. Some consider the psychological traits and characteristics of the individual while others examine family dynamics. Some theories examine the formation of "self" while others adopt a philosophical framework, such as existentialism. The latter theories will be covered in the philosophical section of this book, although it should be noted that these discourses overlap, in that one's philosophical viewpoint, such as belief in mind/body dualism, has a direct bearing on one's psychological framework.

As previously indicated, it is generally accepted that the causes of anorexia are multidimensional, involving interaction among individual, family and societal factors. As its initial onset usually occurs around the time of puberty, he sees it as a phobic avoidance of "growing up", an inability of the individual to face physical, sexual and emotional maturity. In this way, he regards it as a psychologically adaptive state that meets the psychosocial needs of the person, through physical or biological means.

Early theories about anorexia considered the role played by the mother as well as general family dynamics. Some psychoanalytical interpretations of anorexia after the 1930s were based on the premise that eating disorders resulted from an oral disturbance in a child's early years, thus implicating the mother-child relationship. Palazzoli attributed the origin of anorexia to an over-protective mother. However, Palazzoli later adopted a "family-systems" approach, where interactions and communication difficulties in the whole family were implicated.

Families of anorexics were described by researchers as being enmeshed and unable to manage conflict, leading to the concept of a "psychosomatic family". Researchers found that some of the factors indicated earlier, such as enmeshment and rigidity, were contradicted by their own results. Rather, they found that anorexic families demonstrated significantly more emotional distance and expressed more disagreement and dissatisfaction with their familial relationships than control families.

Psychobiological research has isolated many heritable traits or personality dimensions that place someone at risk of developing anorexia. Personality traits that have been associated with the restricting type of anorexia are "emotional restraint, avoidance of novelty, anxious worry and self-doubt, weight–and shape-related anxiety, compliancy, obsessionality, rigidity, over-control, perfectionism and perseverance in the face of no- reward".

These personality phenotypes have been summarised by some researchers as obsessional, inhibited and compliant, while the personality disorders associated with anorexia are avoidant personality disorder, obsessive-compulsive personality disorder, and borderline personality disorder.

These characteristics often predate and remain after the onset of the eating disorder, thus suggesting a predisposition for anorexia.

Characteristics of both anorexia and bulimia nervosa are over-concern with body image and thinness, increased harm avoidance, dysphoria, obsessions about symmetry or exactness and perfectionism. Interestingly, their research indicates that denial of bodily needs is more significant than body dissatisfaction among anorexics. This has also been documented in other research that pinpoints denial and minimization as important factors in anorexia. Whether self-denial is a heritable trait or an environmental response is debatable and will be explored later in this section. Furthermore, the finding that denial of needs is more significant than body dissatisfaction complicates the implications of some of the research discussed earlier, which highlights the effects of media on body dissatisfaction. However, it indicates the complexity of interacting forces in the etiology of anorexia.

Perfectionism and obsessive-compulsiveness have often been linked with anorexia. These traits have also been linked with dieting behavior, which in turn has been linked with anorexia. Parents of anorexic children often describe them in glowing terms, as well-behaved, popular and conscientious, and as high achievers who never appear to experience any satisfaction in their achievements due to an underlying belief that they are never "good enough".

In a study, was found that subjects rated their demands of themselves as being higher than others' expectations but also indicated high demands from family. Perfectionism, which also included compulsivity, was rated very highly as well. Interestingly, this research included follow-ups after eight and sixteen years, providing a longitudinal perspective. In the second follow-up, when asked to rate causal factors of their disorder, family factors were significant. However, it should be noted that this second assessment was likely to have been influenced by other factors, such as treatment received.

A research testimonies signified the importance of obsessive and complex rituals in connection with eating. They analyzed these behaviors using the theory of embodiment which, in this case, refers to the process of grooming the body to better represent the self, as a means of adapting to social interactions. In this construction, a new personality type referred to as the "performing self", emerges and anorexia is posited as a representational illness with image presentation being the primary goal. This performance is enacted in the "theatre" of social relations to maintain face and ward off stress triggered by a threat of failure.

Researchers identify three areas of disordered psychological functioning associated with what she refers to as true anorexia, the first symptom being a disturbance of delusional proportions in the body image and body concept or cachexia. Unless this body concept is corrected, long term improvement is unlikely. The second characteristic is a disturbance in the accuracy of the perception or cognitive interpretation of stimuli arising in the body, including denial of symptoms of hunger or an inability to recognize them. Other falsified interpretations of bodily states are connected to hyperactivity and over-indulgence in exercise, which characterize anorexia.

The anorectic usually denies any fatigue, despite her indulgence in a punishing exercise schedule. Other bodily sensations not readily recognized are changes in temperature and sexual functioning, with many anorexics failing to acknowledge feeling cold and missing cues, such as cramps, before the onset of menstruation. Emotional states are also not identified accurately, causing anxiety and depression to be masked and subsequently not treated for long periods.

The third prominent feature of anorexia, as described by Bruch, is a paralyzing sense of Ineffectiveness and helplessness that dominates the thinking patterns and activities of anorexic patients. In testimonies recorded by Bruch, they describe how they often feel that they are more responsive to the demands of others than to their own needs. However, this is not always recognized as it is often disguised by negativism, defiance, and rejection which, in turn, have developed after a childhood of almost total obedience and over-conformity to parental wishes.

The need for self-reliance and independence may elicit huge conflicts in the anorexic child who, in always acting on the demands and wishes of others, now finds that she must explore her own independence and autonomy. This conflict is often manifested as defiance and obstinacy, but this façade of bravado usually conceals an acute lack of initiative and autonomy brought on by a marked imbalance of power in the relationships between parents and children. The developing child may have felt that she has never been able to exercise any control over her life, with her parents determining every decision and plan made, thereby directing the child in every possible way. The anorexic response can be seen as an individual's attempt to be strong by rising above bodily needs but, ironically, with increasing physical weakness, the anorexic loses the sense of independence and control she so desperately sought.

As mentioned above, descriptions of anorexia often refer to self-denial and, in particular, the denial of emotional and bodily needs. Many theories have been put forward to explain the origin of self-denial.

The relationship between infant and significant caregiver has been central to many of these theories. Early experiences can either consolidate or undermine the infant's sense of trust that his or her physical needs will be met. As the mother is usually the primary caregiver concerning feeding, it is her responsiveness to the infant's cues that becomes integral in developing this sense of trust.

When a mother responds appropriately to her child's needs, the infant learns to trust the mother as well as this reinforcing her own ability to identify sensations of hunger and other appetites. If the mother feeds the infant to suit her own needs and not the child's needs, then this failure to respond to the infant's needs can engender a state of uncertainty in the infant, whereby she becomes unsure about her ability to discriminate inner states and also to be looked after by others.

Furthermore, genetic factors and perinatal injuries may jeopardize the infant's ability to identify body signals of hunger. An infant confused about her own needs is liable to give out indistinct or contradictory clues to her caregiver which, in turn, reinforces the inappropriateness or inadequacy of the responses provided. As a result, the child fails to develop a sense of body identity and experiences difficulty in recognizing hunger and other bodily states. Underlying this argument is the premise that hunger is not necessarily an innate knowledge but a learned construct and that anorexia is indicative of a deficit in a hunger awareness concept.

This inability to discern one's needs may develop into a denial of both emotional and bodily needs. As a result, this may lead to a total denial of "self" that has been described as one of the key factors of anorexia. The link between physical and emotional nurturance has been established in much of the literature about anorexia, with many leading researchers describing the anorexic as emotionally undernourished, an effective analogy given that the anorectic response is to deny physical nourishment.

If a child's needs, especially about food, were not originally fulfilled, she may use self-starving as a means of suppressing an underlying hunger for nurturance. Early histories fail to give evidence of gross neglect but, rather, suggest a subtle interplay between mother and child in terms of appropriateness of response and whether the child's need was interpreted erroneously. Parental availability, either on a physical or emotional level was another key factor. Some anorexics indicated that they felt that their parents were not only unable to understand their emotional needs but were also unavailable on a physical level to meet those needs.

Linked to this inability to fulfill one's needs is a lack of control over one's environment, the third feature indicated by Bruch. Many testimonies given by anorexics indicate that when everything else in their lives seems out of control, dietary intake is the one area that can be controlled. Taken to its extreme, the anorexic may feel she does not have an identity of her own, nor a life of her own, a state of mind that Bruch describes as delusional, given that her identity belongs to her.

Being uncertain of her own needs, the anorexic often focuses on fulfilling her mother's needs to strengthen the connection with her, thereby gaining maternal approval through absolute compliance. This leads to a lack of independence and initiative that compounds her feelings of ineffectiveness and helplessness in the face of bodily urges. Unable to determine her own destiny, she feels controlled from the outside.

Anorexia then becomes a form of rebellion, a desperate fight against feeling "enslaved, exploited and not being permitted to lead a life of their own".

However, while this explanation may hold true in many cases, it does not account for the full range of family backgrounds observed in practice; some, for example, is characterized more by chaos than by rigid expectations. Furthermore, in many cases, the child is rebellious long before the disorder develops. In line with this latter argument, my early characterization of Elizabeth shows her rebelling against her mother's wishes and taking drugs. She is also positioned as someone unsure of her identity and unable to control her external circumstances.

The role of the family in the etiology of anorexia has been the focus of much research. It describes how the family often reinforces societal obsession with thinness. While family backgrounds vary in the narratives, a common belief of anorexics was that they would only be accepted, approved of and loved if they met certain standards of achievement and appearance. This form of conditional love was identified as the main familial factor predisposing an adolescent to anorexia. The way explores the process of the personality splitting into "false" and "true" selves whereby the anorexic adopts the persona of a false self to be approved of and loved. This process prevents her from developing self-esteem or a cohesive identity, as only the false self is accepted.

Through a process of denial and negation, a needless but false self is created. This false self is accepted and validated by significant others and this strengthens the individual's self-esteem. Thus, anorexia is posited as an attempted solution to being in a world that, on a profound and deep level, one feels excluded from and not entitled to enter.

Anorexia is regarded in this interpretation as a defense against dependency needs. Having learned from observing her mother that she will be unable to have her emotional needs met and must instead serve the needs of others, the anorexic overcomes and rejects these needs through her "hunger strike". The "false self" has been extrapolated to the "false body" that the anorexic can change and reshape through self-starvation. The "false body" is positioned as a defense against the real body that is perceived as being unacceptable.

Researchers compare the food obsession of contemporary women with the elements of a rite of passage, as reflected in the mother-daughter separation struggle, but concludes that it fails to accomplish the rite's purpose of moving the individual from one stage of life to the next. They describe the mother-daughter separation struggle and need for identity as entangled in a "hunger knot".

Late 20th century women make up the first generation in history that has the social and psychological opportunities to surpass the life choices made by their mothers but, instead, many of these women are being consumed by eating disorders that prevent them from taking advantage of these opportunities. She refers to statistics that indicate half of campus students suffer from an eating disorder and are constantly battling their hunger. Recent statistics, already discussed, indicate that the situation has not changed considerably. The underlying cause of this struggle is attributed to a serious form of identity crisis. Indeed, she suggests that the current "epidemic" of eating disorders can be understood as a crisis of confusion about the role of women in the modern world after decades of fighting for female liberation. This point has already been raised in explaining the link between feminism and eating disorders. She cites examples of women who describe their feelings of emptiness and lack of a bona fide self, that is, uncertainty about the nature of their identity, similarly described by Betty Friedan, in the 1960s. These women also describe a terror of self-development, evident even among successful women.

This avoidance of growth and development to the conflict experienced by females, who may feel guilty taking up opportunities denied to their mothers. An eating disorder can thus be seen as a way of evading the inner turmoil about surpassing one's mother. The daughter is aware of but unable to acknowledge the inner turmoil experienced by her mother, having sacrificed her own aspirations for her family. Furthermore, if the daughter sensed that her mother was ambivalent about this choice, she may be angry that her mother had betrayed her potential. In her aspiration to develop her own potential, the daughter faces the intolerable position of inciting envy and resentment by reminding her mother of her own failure to achieve what she had once sought.

Caught in this emotional web, the daughter might turn upon herself and the eating disorder could then be viewed as an expression of the guilt, rage, anxiety, and fear of separation from her mother that she is unable to express more directly. Food, being equated with the mother's role from infancy, thus becomes the method of separation from her at the onset of adulthood when the daughter is struggling to express her autonomy. By refusing to eat, the daughter separates symbolically from the mother and isolates herself from the gathering place that represents family cohesion.

The mother-daughter relationship has been the focus of other interpretations of anorexia, one of them being that, in the perception of the maturing child, her mother models her own destiny; while being successful in the eyes of the world, she must also be the feminine, sexual and self-denying mother. This may lead to the daughter aspiring towards high achievement while ensuring that her body remains as thin and non-maternal as possible, in order not to be like her mother.

Researchers refer to the underlying infantile rage over unmet needs and panic about the separation that must be addressed in working with an eating disordered child. One client, referred to as Marie, is so "full up" of anger and rage that she is too full to eat. In this depiction, the child experiences both rage and panic about separating from the primary parental figure. The link between self-starvation and self-harm is also drawn in this depiction with acts of self-harm such as cutting and, in extreme cases, death, being regarded as weapons in the battle for control. Marie's suicide attempts and other forms of self-harm, including her eating disorder, symbolized her sense of her "self" being destroyed but, at the same time, positioned death as a relief from her fear of psychic fragmentation.

The psychological profile of a child with anorexia indicates the development of a pseudo-autonomous self that rejects nurturance, both on an emotional and physical level, thus leaving the inner self starved of understanding and support. Once again, this latter argument reinforces my presentation of Elizabeth's battle for autonomy, even as she remains dependent on her family, and validates the link between self-harm and anorexia depicted in the play.

Some scholars describe anorexia as a type of autistic psychic retreat, resulting from a disruption to the mother-infant bond. An autistic psychic retreat is defined as a defensive withdrawal to a primitive enclosed part of the self that had been damaged by some infantile trauma. This damaged aspect of the self is sectioned or cut-off from the remaining psychic structure and becomes an enclave of autism or pocket of autistic functioning, which basically acts as a defense mechanism.

They present examples of patients to illustrate the types of issues involved; for instance, a girl referred to as Amy, who has never separated from her mother, experiences both extreme dependence and intense hatred of her mother. If Amy eats enough to gain weight, she feels that her mother has won, but if she loses weight, the feeling becomes one of triumph over her mother and symbolizes her control over the "shared" body that represents "her somato-psychic fusion" with her mother. The central significance of control is emphasized again in this narrative which describes how, amid the physical and emotional changes of puberty, the anorexic feels that she is only able to control one thing, that is, her body.

Researchers primarily focuses on the maternal bond, and, in particular, dysfunctional aspects of it. As the mother is often the primary care-giver, especially in infancy, her responsiveness to the child's needs and the role model of womanhood that she provides is regarded as instrumental in shoring up the child's self-identity and self-esteem.

All theorists emphasize the significance of control. I found all their arguments informative and helpful in my depiction of the relationship between Barbara and Elizabeth.

The father's role in the development of anorexia has also received attention. In a recent study, it was found that paternal psychological control may impact adolescent development by hindering, suppressing or preventing the development of emotion regulation abilities, thus contributing to or causing symptoms of eating disorders.

Emotion regulation has been defined as the process that is responsible for monitoring, evaluating and modifying emotional reactions. Paternal psychological control in the form of over-protectiveness was shown to decrease adolescents' abilities to regulate their emotions which, in turn, is associated with eating disorder symptoms. This study further supported an association between the number of proximal adverse life experiences and eating disorder development.

Furthermore, the Parental Bonding Instrument used does not sufficiently differentiate between behavioral and psychological control. However, despite design inadequacies, the study presents evidence that an inability to regulate emotion confers risks in psychological disorders and that intrusive paternal parenting impacted upon these deficits.

Interestingly, research on the daughters of eminent men found several commonalities among women. They were described as bright and talented, with extremely successful fathers in intellectual or political fields but with mothers who were not as successful. All of the women studied had displayed adolescent ailments that included extreme thinness, with some demonstrating depression and disordered eating.

Women who strive to achieve in male-dominated areas but felt restricted in being female had a propensity towards disordered eating. Their sample included high profile figures, such as Indira Gandhi and Queen Elizabeth 1.

In summarising the psychological literature on the roles played by mothers and fathers in eating disorder pathology before 1979, any earlier claim made that the mother is the dominant figure in the anorexic family has not been confirmed by larger studies.

There is no one predominant parental personality profile or type of marital relationship evident in patients' families.

While there are some families with the mother presenting as the dominant influence, the significance of the father's role and his relationship with his wife is also indicated. Consequently, certain types of family conflicts correlate with different onset ages of anorexia. Patients aged 11 to 14 years were more likely to have depressed mothers than those in older age groups. In the older onset age group, they found that personality problems, domineering behavior and ambivalent feelings were characteristic of mothers' profiles. More recent research that has considered the role of fathers in the development of anorexia has referred to a concept of "father hunger".

Alternatively, they retain physical proximity but may, inadvertently, express discomfort about this proximity to their daughters who then withdraw their affections. In both scenarios, the daughter may react subconsciously by retreating to a pre-pubertal state to regain the father's affection and approval. Elizabeth in "Frames" wishes to retreat to an earlier stage of her development before she discovered that her father was having an affair, to regain a trusting relationship with him again. I deliberately chose the age of ten, as it is usually pre-pubertal, and conveys an innocence before she becomes a sexualized figure.

Many family factors have been indicated as risk factors in the development of eating disorders, particularly anorexia. Some of the factors documented are family unpredictability, parental psychopathology and childhood sexual abuse.

While evidence suggests a strong link with parental psychopathology, the impact of family unpredictability is mediated by the supportiveness of family relationships. Research also indicates a higher prevalence of eating disorders among victims of childhood sexual abuse. Given that victims of sexual abuse are often silenced, there is a lack of statistical evidence to prove this association. Sexual abuse can be a precipitating factor and continued abuse or fear of continuing abuse may be a perpetuating factor.

Results are conflicting. Some studies indicate that

over-protectiveness and family enmeshment are significant factors, while other research suggests that less involvement and supportiveness are characteristic. However, one consistent family factor that acts as a deterrent to eating disorders is family support and cohesiveness.

Both mothers and fathers have unique influences on adolescent weight concerns and that parenting strategy that builds intimacy, enhance knowledge of children's daily experiences and effectively resolve conflict act as preventative factors, whereas parent-child relationships that are low in intimacy and high in parental over-control are risk factors.

The assessment of family functioning in anorexic families is fraught with methodological difficulties. Research has indicated that often family functioning in eating disordered families is described as normal by self-report but this is not confirmed by objective measures. In terms of rating family functioning, research indicates that clinicians and patients are both more critical in rating this dimension than parents.

Higher rates of parental discord and higher parental demands have been associated with anorexia, compared with other psychiatric disorders.

Critical comments about weight and shape, along with interpersonal stresses, were associated with an increased risk of anorexia, although these factors were most salient in the twelve months leading up to the onset of anorexia.

Given that half of them were above the age of 18 years, the usual set limit for the assessment of parenting variables, there was a lack of corroborating evidence from other family members. Chance remarks about weight and shape, often meant innocuously, can act as a trigger for dieting, which research has shown to be a strong risk factor for anorexia.

In terms of other family factors, while there is no evidence to support the characteristics of enmeshment and inability to manage conflict, proposed as risk factors, empirical evidence indicates that families who manifest dysfunctional interaction, with poor communication, conflict, and inconsistency between parents, have a higher incidence of anorexia. It is frequently the case in anorexic families that "feelings are denied, ignored, denigrated or dismissed" and the child with the eating disorder often sits between the parents, suggesting that she may provide a buffer between them or exercise a significant amount of control over them, possibly being the center of their attention.

Less clear is whether these patterns predate the onset or are a reaction to the disorder. It seems that there are many methodological difficulties in establishing causal links between family factors and anorexia, due to limitations in measurement devices and the difficulties associated with obtaining corroborating evidence from other family members.

Other factors that may be relevant to anorexia are more profound life events, such as, illness, change of school, moving house, bereavement and other adverse life changes. In "Frames", Elizabeth's anorexia becomes more severe and noticeable after the family has moved house, suggesting that this move could have hurt her.

Alternate theories about anorexia delve into the meaning of what eating represents to the subgroup of anorexics who are not so concerned with weight gain but who experience a sense of horror about eating. It has been postulated that some anorexics, also described as secondary anorexia, have a deep-seated fear of death and view food as a reminder of death, given that eating generally involves consumption of dead animals or plants. In this framework, the anorexic can be conceptualized as somewhere between life and death, both too afraid to live fully and too afraid to die. The connection between anorexia and suicide has been previously indicated, with anorexia being regarded as self-destructive behavior and also as a gradual form of suicide.

In treating anorexia, a collaborative approach to therapy among professionals is recommended, with family therapy and, more recently, the Maudsley method, which includes the family as a resource in treatment, being the preferred choice of treatment. However, there is some inconsistency among professionals about the efficacy of family-based treatments compared to inpatient treatment.

Overall, treatments that promote an active role for parents in tackling anorexia appear to be more effective than those that only encourage a supportive role. Given inconsistent research findings of the role played by the family in the etiology of eating disorders, there has been a conceptual shift away from treating family dynamics as causative to regarding them as maintenance mechanisms. By taking a non-blaming approach to the family and regarding them as a resource in treatment, family interventions have moved towards focusing on re-feeding and this indirectly changes family dynamics to aid in recovery.

To conclude, there is no single family cause for the development of the disorder. Rather, research indicates that families fall on a continuum from optimal functioning to highly dysfunctional. While there are some common elements, such as the anorexic's need to establish autonomy and control, family backgrounds remain diverse. There is also a need to study the process by which Western culture's emphasis on slimness is transmitted through the family. Furthermore, it is necessary to consider individual responses when studying this process.

My review of psychological literature provided support for the approach that I had taken when writing the first draft of "Frames", but also helped shape the way the play was re-written. I tried to stress the anorexic need for control, while also depicting identity confusion and low self-esteem. I chose a scenario that demonstrates a moderate level of family dysfunction, as opposed to one that is more extreme, because I felt that this would be more representative and resonate more broadly to audiences. I also wanted to show the processes by which Western cultural values are transmitted through the family, by positioning Barbara in a form of media that often promotes a slender-ideal and by showing focus on female slimness and attractiveness. I also characterized Elizabeth by portraying qualities of perfectionism, such as the hand-painting incident referred to earlier and obsessiveness as shown by her extreme exercising.

A philosophical frame, including religious, spiritual and cultural factors

Anorexia and other eating disorders, encapsulate what is wrong with our current culture. Her claim is supported by epidemiological data indicating that anorexia has become highly prevalent among women in contemporary society. Therefore, it is imperative to discover what is missing from our culture at this historical juncture to understand more fully the spiritual and philosophical dimensions of women's troubled relationship with food.

By adopting a philosophical frame, it becomes possible not only to examine some of the paradigms or discourses that are employed to understand this phenomenon but also to consider the nature of these discourses themselves and to establish how the type of discourse employed determines the type of knowledge that can be gathered. Some of the discourses already covered, such as the medical approach, have been shown to position anorexia according to the medical terminology and dominant ideas of historical periods. In the late 1800s, for example, anorexia was described as "hysterical" in keeping with the dominant paradigm of this period.

A philosophical perspective dominating European culture has been the construct of dualism, first espoused by Plato. The dualistic perspective makes a distinction between body and mind or body and spirit.

In contrast, the true self, whether conceived as mind, spirit, soul or just as "not-body" represents the best, highest, noblest aspects of humanity and all that is closest to God. This conception of mind/body separateness led, on a theological level, to regarding the physical side of human nature as impure and sinful, always dragging down the aspiring spirit, and as an obstacle to the inner self.

According to a theological perspective, moral perfection can only be achieved by subduing or rising above the flesh. The experience of the body, as the center of existence, described as embodiment, allows us to feel alive.

However, this also means that our embodied perspective is subjective since we cannot view things independently of our "lived-in" experience. To gain a more objective viewpoint, we would need to adopt a disembodied perspective, that is, a perspective from outside of our bodies, something that we may wish but find difficult to achieve! The anorexic rejects her bodily needs and strives to transcend the limitations of the flesh. In many ways, she would like to become disembodied.

The Greeks regarded body and soul as inseparable except in death, while Descartes believed that it was possible to transcend the body. The famous Cartesian statement "I think, therefore I am" encapsulates the mind/body dualism in European culture. A dualistic approach separates the experience of mind from body, creating a split within the individual and, interestingly, this resonates with the experiences portrayed by many anorexics in their narratives.

A feminist perspective of dualism clearly indicates that it is also gendered, with women cast in the role of body while man is constructed as mind, intellect and absolute spirit.

Women's bodies have also been regarded as impure, unclean and dangerous, meaning that they must be overcome if women are to pursue moral worthiness. Some women come to believe that they must somehow dissociate from their bodies. Rather than the alternative conceptualization of their bodies as natural or miraculous, they come to fear them as uncontrollable, alien and evil. If a woman is conceived as a body and the body is perceived as a negative object, then it follows that women may be conceptualized as negative.

It has been argued that the anorexic may take the dualism of body and spirit literally. In other words, the anorexic's need to limit and control her food intake may represent a moral striving and an attempt to prove that she is morally and spiritually worthy. Believing that her body and her self are two distinct and separate entities allows her to abuse her body for a greater good.

Some theorists have argued that the destructive and often obsessive relationship many women have with their bodies is an internalization of our patriarchal society's conceptualization of women's bodies, incorporating both contempt and worship simultaneously.

This results in women battling to overcome antagonism towards their bodies to perfect them so that they may be "worshipped" instead. Such a fixation on the body leads more to a state of disembodiment than embodiment, as body hatred and narcissism still posit the body as separate to self. Body image, as outlined earlier, is a product of one's imagination and, as such, is distinct from the actual physical body and the image that outside observers have of the body.

Twentieth-century existentialists such as Jean-

Paul Sartre and Simone de Beauvoir, as well as philosophers such as Derrida, Dewey, and Foucault, attempted to eliminate body/mind dualism. Sartre and de Beauvoir attempted to transcend the body, rather than integrate both aspects of "self" and conceptualized the body in various ways as "body-in-itself", "body-for-others", and "body for myself as known by the other".

The latter concept suggests that we can only know ourselves through the eyes of others and how they perceive us. Sartre describes the alienation and longing for invisibility produced by this state of being. Interestingly, the testimonies of many anorexics describe a similar emotional state. Simone de Beauvoir influenced the development of a feminist discourse of the female body and the oppression of women. Her account describes the dialectic in both the individual and in the broader culture, where the male is regarded as the norm or positive subject, while the female is defined only about the male and thus becomes the inessential object, creating an opposition between male subject and female object.

Thus, a woman's identity is defined by her status as "other" and a woman's body is defined by its reproductive capacity. In a patriarchal culture, it can be argued that the woman becomes alienated from her body, as the body is not regarded as the subject that gives meaning but rather as the object of a masculine cultural viewpoint.

Other feminist theorists have drawn from psychoanalytic theory, such as that postulated by Freud, to support their arguments.

An analysis of the feminist construction of female identity reinforces the Foucauldian position that discourses construct, to some extent, the reality that they describe. When defined about the male, the female has been constructed as a negative entity, lacking or deficient in fundamental ways. This viewpoint has permeated cultural beliefs and has been inculcated into women's beliefs about themselves so that they construct their own reality from the perspectives presented by the dominant patriarchal order. Consequently, it is important to consider all academic and clinical texts about anorexia as discourses that actively construct certain realities through their descriptions.

Anorexia has also been positioned as a metaphor for sociocultural concerns, such as the conflict between mass consumption and normative thinness. Consumer capitalism, which relies on the production of novel images, has created images of femininity that exalt slenderness and beauty. These representations both homogenize, that is, smooth out all racial, ethnic and sexual differences, as well as normalize, thereby encouraging women constantly to compare and judge themselves against standardized images that promote a particular look, which varies across cultures, and urges them to use cosmetic surgery and other means to meet these standards.

The dualist axis that began with Plato and was consolidated by Descartes clearly separates the bodily or material from the mental or spiritual aspects of human existence. By adopting this philosophical stance, the body is experienced as an alien (the not-me) and as a form of confinement or prison from which the soul is constantly struggling to escape.

It is also regarded as an enemy that sabotages our thinking by filling us with lusts, fears, and fancies, as well as being prone to diseases that undermine our health. Finally, it is seen as an impediment to reason, and so threatens our attempts at control. However, the more we attempt to subdue or control bodily desires and hunger, the more we constitute them as alien and powerful, setting up a no-win vicious circle. The only way to overcome this problem is to go beyond control and cease to experience these hunger and desires, which is what many anorectics describe as their ultimate goal. Many narratives indicate an obsession with hunger as much as an obsession with slimness, but this hunger is experienced as an alien invader that is not part of themselves. This is akin to earlier descriptions that indicate anorexics experience all bodily sensations as foreign.

Associated with this is the experience of the soul or will be imprisoned in the body, with many narratives describing the desire to escape the body or to exist without a body. The thin body or non-body represents a triumph of will over the body and transcendence of the flesh associated with impurity and mental decay. Once again, we see parallels between fasting medieval saints and modern-day anorexics; as discussed earlier, the saints tried to subdue or transcend the body.

The control axis refers to the anorectic experience of feeling that her life and her hunger are out of control. By exercising control over her body she can exercise some control over her life. While there is a high morbidity rate among anorexics, the dominant experience is one of invulnerability.

On the gender/power axis, the anorectic's

distorted image of her body can be regarded as an extreme case of a common female misperception. With society's glamorization of the thin body and the pressure on women to have a body that conforms to the romantic or sexual ideal, it is no wonder that women constantly overestimate their size.

The thin body in this conceptualization signifies a cultural rejection of the feminine but paradoxically works in collusion with the very cultural conditions that produce this ideal. In this way, anorexics both reject and embody traditional patriarchal gender identities. Despite pursuing conventional feminine behavior in the form of extreme dieting, the anorexic can be seen to deconstruct conventional femininity at its extreme point as she then highlights those values that are coded as male in our society.

On a broader level, the body represents both a counterpoint and a metaphor for mind and spirit in this dualistic framework. The anorexic body symbolizes the mind's triumph over the body and at its extreme point may also be construed as a form of dematerialization of the body in that the person may experience a sense that the body ceases to exist, allowing the person to feel a disembodied "spiritual" subjectivity.

This representation positions the anorexic's subjectivity as strong and powerful and signifies the "self" as a controlled entity. In this sense, the dualist discourse differs significantly from Christian asceticism, which exalts a complete renunciation of the self. Hence, a dualistic reading constitutes self- starvation as self-productive as opposed to self-destructive. It also signifies a transcendence of femininity, as a thin anorexic body represents a subjectivity that is essentially the antithesis of the body and is thus genderless.

In this way, the thin anorexic body is constituted as a controlled body indicating a powerful, disembodied and genderless position. As already mentioned, the dualist discourse positions "woman" as body and bodily excess. In this conceptualization, she is the antithesis of the mind/self, thus depicting "woman" in the extreme representation as "woman-too-much". This gives rise to other constructions of "woman" as talking too much, being too emotional and needy and taking up too much space. When a dualistic discourse converges with a patriarchal and misogynistic framework, a damaging construction of "woman" as uncontrollable, disruptive and essentially as the Other is consolidated.

In this light, the anorexic position of taking up less space, eating less and rising above bodily needs may be seen as the ideal. The Cartesian discourse, by consolidating a negative construction of "woman", can be interpreted as producing the desire to control and ultimately eradicate the female body, thus leading to the widespread cultural practice whereby women engage in a process of bodily destruction through self-starvation.

An analysis of these different discourses reveals the multiplicity of meanings that the thin anorexic body represents. It may be viewed as conforming to the social norms of femininity and may also be construed as androgynous or boyishly thin. It may be regarded as small and childlike or as signifying a powerful and disembodied subjectivity. Ultimately, it may be seen as both a symbol of self-production and a form of self-destruction. Many anorexic narratives position anorexia in a positive construction as a search for identity, the corollary being that without anorexia the individual has no identity.

In her quest to produce an identity, the anorexic is at the same time destroying herself on both a literal and metaphorical level. In one construction, the self is regarded as defective and unworthy, deserving punishment and, in this regard, not eating is a way of inflicting self-harm or self-punishment.

Cultural attitudes towards the body also reflect the fragmented and contradictory nature of our times. As postulated by some theorists, our culture seems to espouse biological determinism, with genetic and chemical accounts presented for a diverse range of psychological disorders, and also cultural constructionism, with the body being inscribed and shaped by culture. Biomedical explanations of anorexia, which signify the importance of dysfunctional hormones, can in some ways be regarded as both sexist and reductionist, as they assume a concept of objective truth that is, in itself, problematic.

Medical and psychological discourses can thus be interpreted on a philosophical level to construct anorexia in particular ways, rather than simply to describe a disorder. The feminist view that the body is a cultural form has been supported by poststructuralist perspectives, such as the Foucauldian view that prevailing power dynamics are constantly transforming to produce new forms of subjectivity.

Religious, spiritual and cultural factors

In contemporary times, in Western democracies, religious questions about the meaning of life have been left to the individual or have been reduced and commodified in a consumer-capitalist context. Many theorists have drawn comparisons between the fanaticism demonstrated by girls in pursuit of the perfect body and religious fanaticism, with some calling the pursuit of slenderness the "new religion", while others draw parallels with religious cults.

The spiritual hunger associated with anorexia has been attributed to the embodied effects of living in a society that is still driven to some extent by "dualism and domination: of spirit over body, men over women, thought over feeling, white over colored, individual over community, rich over poor". In this context, anorexia can be understood as a crisis of meaning, as a symbolic, ritualizing attempt to construct hope and fill a void in a dominant culture that leaves many women feeling a sense of emptiness and meaninglessness.

While traditional Christianity may have associated women's appetites and bodily cravings with sin into the world, as an interpretation of the Adam and Eve biblical story, and the consequent need to transcend bodily needs to be saved. However, traditional Christianity, with its history of female oppression and marginalization, would need to transform itself away from these legacies to provide the spiritual nourishment that is needed by women today.

Modern science has shifted the focus from the state of one's soul to the state of the body as a reflector of one's inner state. By promoting slender ideals, a symbolic ideal is actually being inculcated.

However, while this new religion promises redemption and salvation, it fails to deliver any meaning other than a superficial one to its followers; even so, for women struggling with confusion, injustice, anxieties, and longings, daily rituals can become extremely significant. In following them, however, as it is not just weight that is lost, but faith, trust, and hope to compound their sense of emptiness, alienation, powerlessness, and despair. The desire to transcend the physical and the limits of female life and to enter the male-defined sphere of ideas and thought is often expressed in narratives by anorexics. By entering this world, they can escape the vulnerability and needs of embodiment.

The salvation myth promised by anorexia needs

to be taken into account in any explanation of the illness. Hunger for a sense of fulfillment and well-being drives the anorexic's struggle and, in this sense, starving becomes a means not only to achieve "wellness" but also a sense of salvation.

While many standardized psychological tests and structured assessment techniques, as well as questionnaires, have been developed to ascertain psychosocial and medical correlates of anorexia, none of them adequately assesses religious and spiritual aspects of functioning and their relationship to eating pathology. Faith and spirituality form a significant aspect of many people's lives and should be considered for the following reasons: to better understand and empathize with patients' worldviews; to ascertain whether the patient's religious-spiritual orientation is having a detrimental effect on them or whether their belief system can be mustered as a resource to help them and, if so, which spiritual interventions would be appropriate; and, finally, whether patients have unresolved spiritual doubts, needs or concerns.

They further identified the following dimensions as being significant in working with eating disorders: metaphysical worldview, religious affiliation, religious orthodoxy, religious problem-solving style, spiritual identity, God-image, value-lifestyle congruence, doctrinal knowledge, and spiritual maturity. Therapists can use information gleaned from this type of assessment to uncover and clarify hopes and desires about how their patients would like their spiritual life to be, to use these as goals and also to find out what patients are placing their faith in; for instance, women with an eating disorder often place their faith in this eating disorder. With this knowledge, the authors argue, the therapist can help them to place their faith in themselves, God, others who love them or their future, as a strategy to shift their faith from the eating disorder.

Other research has uncovered ten false beliefs shared by eating disordered women that prevent them from genuinely connecting with other people and with God. These beliefs are listed as:

- the eating disorder will provide control of life and emotions
- the eating disorder will effectively communicate pain and suffering
- the eating disorder will make the person exceptional in both a "better than" and "worse than" others manner
- the eating disorder proves that the person is bad

and unworthy and deserving of punishment

- the eating disorder will bestow perfection, by having self-control over their bodies, and will make up for other areas of perceived imperfection
- the eating disorder gives comfort and safety from pain, although temporarily only
- the eating disorder provides a sense of identity
- the eating disorder compensates or atones for the past
- the eating disorder allows avoidance of personal responsibility for one's life
- the eating disorder bestows approval from others.

By identifying the beliefs that are dominating their clients' thought processes, therapists can help challenge these beliefs and replace them with healthier ones. They have also found prayer, consistent with a client's religious tradition, to be positively associated with healing, well-being, and happiness. Harnessing the healing potential of clients' faith and spirituality is an important part of the recovery process.

An anthropological frame

As discussed in earlier chapters, anorexia has typically been regarded as a Western cultural illness or Western Culture-Bound Syndrome (CBS), generated by cultural values, beliefs, and social organizations and, as such, it focuses attention on the central ills of our culture. Therefore, a reading of the meaning of bodies becomes a complex matter, given the differences inculcated by race, class, gender, and ethnicity.

However, mass cultural representations that typify Western society have a homogenizing effect by smoothing out all racial, ethnic and sexual differences, promoting instead the expected and usual Anglo-Saxon image. Alternative images that employ different models, such as African American, are re-framed as exotic or are selected based on how well they conform to light-skinned, Anglo-featured models, thereby setting limits on the validation of "difference". Routinely, female role models alter their appearance, through cosmetics or cosmetic surgery to conform to the dominant image society venerates and, in so doing, they iron out differences due to their ethnicity and cultural background.

Once we move away from this homogenizing

Western cultural image, we find a diversity of images that are shaped by ethnic, national, historical and class parameters, to name but a few. As previously outlined, the earlier Anglo-Saxon model of beauty was more buxom with numerous portraits and paintings exalting a voluptuous appearance and people from Greek, Italian, Eastern Europe and of African descent considered this more fleshy look appealing.

While Western culture also promotes a buxom and voluptuous appearance, fashion magazines, which arguably have a strong influence on young women, favor the slender frame. Of course, it should also be noted that historical paintings and portraits do not necessarily ascribe value and meaning to what they depict, so it is difficult to accurately interpret what these paintings and portraits tell us about their culture. Poverty has also had a profound effect on considerations of feminine beauty with body size becoming a signifier of social status in countries such as India and Africa, where thinness is often associated with deprivation and lower socioeconomic status.

There is considerable evidence linking increased rates of anorexia with ever- diminishing slender ideals portrayed by Western cultural models. Until recently, the specificity in the distribution of diagnoses of anorexia in terms of ethnicity and socioeconomic class indicated a strong cultural influence. However, with the proliferation of Western cultural values across diverse ethnic backgrounds and socioeconomic class, anorexia is becoming more prevalent across all socioeconomic and ethnic backgrounds with research indicating that eating attitude is correlated with degree of acculturation to these Western thin-ideals.

There is a near-universal vulnerability to eating disorders and body image concerns. In societies of extreme poverty, anorexia is not a significant problem. Furthermore, as has been previously suggested, anorexia may be understood as expressing a cultural conflict between mass consumption and normative thinness, between the indulgent "consumer-self" and the more controlled "producer-self" as portrayed in a capitalist framework. If linked in this way to consumption and capitalism, then anorexia may be construed as a CBS with roots in Western cultural values and conflicts.

Cultural definitions of social roles also impact eating disorders, as cultures in which women have a restricted role, such as some patriarchal Islamic societies, are associated with lower rates of eating disorders. Researches indicate that societies in which female choice and freedoms are extremely limited have virtually no incidences of anorexia. On the other end of the spectrum, cultures that encourage women to be assertive, self-directed and active publicly as well as within the family, such as African-American and Jewish cultures, engender independence in women that is not consistent with eating problems. However, some research has shown that anorexia is beginning to cross the socioeconomic and cultural divide, appearing in diverse cultures from Africa to the far East.

With the expanding globalization of communication technology, anorexia is now considered to be more linked with the culture of modernity, characterized by an internationalized socioeconomic stratum, increased affluence, universal "fatphobia" and a dissemination of biomedical technology that has, ironically, helped to propagate the condition through measures that were intended to prevent it.

Other cross-cultural research, indicates that eating disorder symptoms reflect more about an adolescent's struggle to adapt to a rapidly changing society than just the adoption of Western cultural beauty standards. The rising incidence of eating disorders appears to be linked to a shift in young people's sense of identity, moving from family and relationships with the community to a greater focus on self and the body.

Narratives that challenge the notion that anorexia is a mental illness, recontextualize anorexia in terms of normalcy, beginning with a normal diet and proceeding to an ascetic phase in which pleasant aspects of starvation are experienced, that is, feelings of independence, emancipation, specialness, and power. The dialectical nature of hunger means that it is experienced as both painful and pleasurable, thereby positing the overcoming of hunger in the Israeli cultural context as an act of heroism.

This is reinforced by narratives that compare the anorexic experience with that of the soldier fighting to survive in difficult circumstances, where "self-inflicted hunger is experienced as a heroic way of being in the world". Gooldin argues that anorexia would be experienced and understood differently in other cultures, such as Japan and Mexico, and it is, therefore, crucial to use an ethnographic approach to understand the meaning of anorexia in diverse cultures and to bridge the gap between anorexic narratives and feminist epistemologies.

From an anthropological viewpoint, a construction of femininity and gender must consider the effects of race, class, ethnicity and sexual orientation in understanding eating disorders. By analyzing how diverse populations of women deal with body image issues and eating problems, we can gain a broader perspective of the social conditions and inequalities that lead many women to regard eating disorders as the "logical" solution to more deep-seated social problems.

It has been argued that some health issues are systemic issues with economic, political and social dimensions on a regional, national and global level, thus demanding systemic solutions.

Conclusion

Anorexia nervosa is a severe eating disorder that is characterized as a mental illness. In some cases, it can lead to death. Whether the patient is influenced by biological factors or sociocultural factors, the outcome is the same: thin and unhealthy.

A personality change is a very common side effect of anorexia among teenage girls. In most cases, she becomes less outgoing and less fun to be with. This leads to her distancing herself from her friends, and she may seem to lose interest in everything except food and academics.

Also, the girl may become more organized and obsessive. She may also want to cook for the family and even encourage them to eat. Although these traits may have existed before the onset of anorexia, "they are usually accentuated by the disorder."

Another common side effect of anorexia is the change in family relationships. Teenage girls suffering from anorexia have been known to "lose confidence and become less assertive, less argumentative, and more dependent." The aforementioned personality changes are a warning sign to parents because teenagers are notorious for trying to be independent and being very argumentative.

Sometimes anorexia can go unnoticed for too long, due to the girl being able to deceive her parents. Such deceptions could take the form of hiding food at the dinner table or worse, bulimia.

Bulimia is a disease, also mainly affecting teenage girls, in which a girl will eat a normal meal but, immediately afterward, regurgitate it. Often coupled with anorexia because it is an easy way for a teenage girl to trick her parents into thinking that she is eating normally, bulimia is a serious threat. It can cause such bad side effects as tooth decay and bleeding within the throat.

Although anorexia is a serious and harmful condition, there are treatment options available. One option is therapy. Most often, the girl is keeping her feelings inside and that is what is making her depressed and, in turn, anorexic.

All she may need is for someone to listen to her problems and offer some good advice. Therapy works well for cases in which the underlying problems may be fairly direct and easy to discuss and treat. However, if the problems are not easy to discuss or the girl refuses to go to therapy, other methods of treatment are available.

CPSIA information can be obtained
at www.ICGtesting.com
Printed in the USA
LVHW051045211120
672146LV00005B/546

9 781801 186391